Oh my god, what shall I call my book?

Danielle James

BookLeaf
Publishing

Presentation by *BookLeaf Publishing*

Web: www.bookleafpub.com

E-mail: info@bookleafpub.com

ISBN: 9789357740043

First edition 2023

To Roy, my muse.

ACKNOWLEDGEMENT

Thank you to my family and non existent friends. This book would have been possible without you.

PREFACE

"Do not go gentle into that good night,
Old age should burn and rave at close of day;
Rage, rage against the dying of the light."

Dylan Thomas.

Toothache is worse than heartbreak

Sugar is the deadliest drug of all and is
responsible for my current crisis,
I'd even go so far as to say it's just as bad as
ISIS.
Mango loco, mango loco, it's made me go mad
and loco.
My teeth scream out in pain, there's absolutely
nothing to gain.
Black and throbbing and rotten, the dentists
advice is quickly forgotten.
I want to rip each individual tooth out, inside I
scream, inside I shout.
Go to Turkey and get some veneers, but it's the
shaven teeth that is my only fear.
But after a tough day at work there's only one
thing I crave.
It's big and it's blue and my day it could save.
Get home, throw my keys on the windowsill.
Open the fridge door, ring a ding ding.
There she stands in her ice cold glory, we all
know the end to this story.
Crack it open, chuck in a straw, take a sip and
then one more.

I reach the end of the can and feel dead inside,
my sugar addiction has hurt my pride.
Mango loco, mango loco. Will I ever stop, yo I
don't know....

Food glorious food

I want the perfect body, have done for years and
years.
There's just one thing that's getting in the way,
it's my not ears.
I love food so much, I don't discriminate.
White black or beige, you'll find it on my plate.
My favourite is a Chinese, just rice and chips,
quite bland.
And I'll come out carrying some popadoms in
my hand.
I wouldn't say no to a dinner, chicken, mash and
peas.
But don't forget the yorkshires, just four will do
for me.
Then there's Dominos pizzas, outrageously
overpriced.
But the pepperoni doughballs and cookies are
just so bloody nice.
And then there's the humble chip, my god it goes
with anything.
Sausage, gravy, fish or burgers but never in the
bin.

Emergency

Please help me, it's an emergency.
You are currently in our queue, number 333.
Please help me, it's an emergency.
Have a look at our resources, there is plenty
there to see.
Please help me, it's an emergency.
You cannot call us unless there is an urgency.
Please help me, it's an emergency.
We cannot help, we have no currency.
Please help me, it's an emergency.
Is it absolutely? Do you require surgery?
Please help me, it's an emergency.....
Never mind, she's dead.

Spring in Swansea

The day is sunny and bright.
It feels like spring has sprung.
There's still a chill in the air.
But it's okay I've wrapped up warm.
A few clouds lurk in the sky.
Music is playing nearby.
People popping into Lidls.
It's a Sunday, they're picking up their groceries.
Llansamlet is where we are.
It's not too near, it's not too far.
Taking the dog for a walk.
Gets me out of the house.

Wet

Wet like the rain.
Wet like the puddles that form.
Wet like condensation.
Wet like ink.
Wet like salty tears.
Wet like the fisherman.
Wet like a fish tank.
Wet like the flood.
Wet like oil.
Wet like a washing line.
Wet like a mop.
Wet like sweat running down my back.
Wet like a nervous man.
Wet inside that sacred place, all down to you.

28 February

His name is Roy. He's a Jack Russell boy.
He hates people and dogs, and don't half produce
some logs.
A greedy guts but not really. He's just got an
unfortunate pot belly.
Very sparse hair with some blackheads under
there.
Smoky kohl liner, his eyes could not be finer.
A nose that twitches, an ear that's had stitches.
Breath like death. Stealth over wealth.
He loves sweet things, cupcakes and party rings.
Got a harness in every colour and is adored by
my mother.
Misunderstood, he wants to be good.
But never look him in the eye, for you would
surely die.
He's one in a million, wouldn't change him for a
billion.
Even though he's so naughty, he's the perfect
boy to me.

Nowhere man

Who knows how his life started, this poor
unfortunate soul.
All skin and bones with missing teeth, sinking
into a black hole.
The boy could not settle, where did he belong?
It gave him an idea, he would put it into song.
So he went to the music shop and bought a
saxophone.
If he could master this instrument he would
never be alone.
He started on street corners, a tupperware and a
sign.
Into that saxophone he blew, and soon began to
shine.
That's it, he'd caught the bug and back to the
music shop he went.
A drum set, guitar and keyboard. The boy sure
was intent.
The pavements became a thing of the past and
soon he was filling stadiums.
His most prestigious gig was in front of the
Queen at the London palladium.
Then, one night in Soho he was introduced to
some shiny DJ decks.

For just an hour behind his booth he could earn a
nice fat cheque.
But he soon retired of that lifestyle, stardom was
not for him.
He was fed up of the paparazzi photographing
his unfortunately saggy chin.
He now resides in Swansea, in a village called
Heol Camlan.
Strange to think that this old boy used to be a
nowhere man.

Cuppa

Cup of tea on the daily.
Under any circumstances.
Past.
Present.
Always with sugar.

L.I.F.E.

Life is a funny old thing.
Just as it ends it starts to begin.
Plenty of time to make mistakes.
But when the fog finally clears it's apparently
too late.
Do as I say, not as I do.
But where does doing that get you?
Afraid to walk before you can run.
Until the day you are setting like the sun.
Live life with no regrets is well intentioned
advice.
But what is a regret, can you be more precise?
Scared of getting old, want to be forever young.
The day that it all ends is the day it will begun.

Bad education

We start off at nursery, then reception then
primary.
And then the dreaded comprehensive, maybe
college, maybe university.
But what does it truly matter, what you learned
or what you know.
Reading books and taking classes isn't the only
way to grow.
You can be educated in kindness, in empathy
and through culture.
Or maybe you have learned every single species
of vultures.
It is considered desirable to have this grand old
education.
But I doubt it can help a starving African nation.
So save yourself the bother and put down the
books, shut down the screens.
You are not a machine that is made for that
routine.

This girl

Born on the 4th of March.
Her name was Danielle.

An instant legend.
She continues to thrive.
Her music taste is second to none.
Her driving is phenomenal.
As wise as an owl.
Her talents are endless.

If only everyone could be born on the 4th
March.
And be called Danielle.

An Ode to Roy

We're not going in Go Outdoors Tinks.
You are such a nag!
I'm fed up of polishing that pukka!
Where's your nan?
Right Tinks, get away from there.
You are such a lucky dabber.
You are obsessed with those smelly bones.
Why haven't you eaten your breakfast?
Do you enjoy anything?
Quintessential child.

I look up at the sky, my eyes are squinting.
It's bright, it's blue.
There's a few clouds here and there.
The temperate is warm with a slight chill in the
air.
Traffic is quite busy for a Sunday afternoon.
Squinting as I go, walking along the pavement.
Walking along Bran Close.
The air filling my lungs.
A crow flies through the trees.
People are going on their way in their cars.
Broom broom broom.
I wonder where they are going.

Mamin

You've always hated your teeth, I have no idea
why.
Often described as shy and so quiet but it's
honestly not a bad thing.
For you are a far nicer human being than the
majority of the human race.
Your favourite type of dogs are Greyhounds,
suppose you quite resemble them.
A stoic vegan, such an admirable lifestyle
choice.
Your only flaw is your love of reality television,
it is slowly rotting your brain.
Although I am not sure you even have one.
My partner in crime, although you are a law
abiding citizen.
One day the world will wake up to your great
self.
Thank you for being my lifelong sidekick.
I would never make it without you.

Carlton Superkings

Cigarettes, fags, whatever you wanna call them.
It started one day with an utterly wrong un.

I thought it would stop. It was never meant to
last.
Then all of a sudden 5 years have passed.

Something to do when you're bored or once
you've eaten.
Or to get out of that awkward conversation with
a guy from Nuneaton.

POV

I don't believe in multiple genders for there is
only two.
I do believe in racism, it's everywhere you look.
I think the prisons are overcrowded, we should
just kill them all.
I don't believe in Governments, we are all equal
beings.
I believe in being kind to animals.
Anxiety and depression are used as excuses, get
an actual grip.
Suicide is not that sad, stop talking and just do
it.
Drink if you wanna, sleep if you wanna, fuck if
you wanna.
Whatever you do, you will always piss someone
off.
Because the world is full of snowflakes.
Climate change is a farce, or is it?
I don't know enough and I don't care enough.
I won't be around to see it all go to hell.
So burn your fossils, mine your oils.
Just do what you can when you can if you can.

Gratitude

Thank you for the memories.
Thank you for the gifts.
Thank you for the company.
Thank you for the trips.
Thank you for the money.
Thank you for a place to stay.
Thank you for feeding me.
Thank you for knowing me.
Thank you for giving me life.

Thank you for the music.
For giving it to me.

Species of Origin

Birds are pretty.
Cats are elegant.
Rats are persecuted.
Dogs are sensational.
Horses are boring.
Monkeys are fascinating.
Frogs are rare.
Snails are annoying.
Slugs are pointless.
Elephants are slow.
Dolphins are shiny.
Flies are a nuisance.
Penguins are cold.
Rabbits are cute.
Crocodiles are scary.
Spiders are ugly.
Chickens have a hard time.
Sheep are so nervous.
Snakes are long.
Foxes are elusive.
Hedgehogs are spiky.
Walrus are unattractive.
Goats are chatty.
Pigs suffer.
Pandas are monochrome.

Tigers are majestic.
Humans are wankers.

9 789357 740043